The Magic Book Of Cadabra

Kaidius Kaid

KAIDIUS KAID

THE MAGIC BOOK OF CADABRA

Published by: Kaidius Kaid

website:http://www.kaidiuskaid.com

email: kaidiuskaid@gmail.com

https://twitter.com/kaidiuskaid

Cover Design by: Mahii_creations

Interior Design: Fiona Williams

A CIP record for this book is available from the Library of Congress Cataloging-in-Publication Data.

HARDBACK ISBN: 978-1-7395122-0-0

PAPERBACK ISBN: 978-1-7395122-3-1

DIGITAL ISBN: 978-1-7395122-2-4

Distributed by: Lulu Press, INC

to someone whom I love very much

“Religion is for people scared of going to hell. Spirituality is for people who have already been there.”

Abracadabra.

Allow Those That Have Eyes to See.

Allow Those That Have Ears to Listen.

Allow Those With A Mouth to Speak.

Let Those With A Pen Write.

Abracadabra

Let’s begin. Colour me in.

In my earliest memory that I can recall, before I was even born, I found myself in a special place. It was like I existed in a time before my own birth. I was sitting on the lap of a kind god. It was a magical scene that resembled an alchemist's library with many books and magical objects.

The godly figure was like a gentle Santa Claus, and he had an extraordinary magic mirror. Looking into the mirror, I saw glimpses of different dimensions and realities. In a soft and kind voice, the god spoke to me. He said, "You can choose any life you want from the mirror and live it the way you like. It's time to start your journey of life."

Without much thought, I eagerly expressed my desire to become a god like him. But god warned me that this path would be filled with dangers, as I would later discover. The next thing I remember is waking up in a twin steel pram next to my six-month-old brother. It was in the middle of 1964, and we were parked near a bustling fruit and vegetable stall at the local market. The sight of the colourful fruits, the plump bananas fascinated me.

Excitedly, I reached out to grab a banana, but my mother quickly took it from my hands and put it back.

I was puzzled and let out a loud cry of protest. Later, I remember jumping up and down on the living room sofa, pestering my mother to let me go outside. I was only about two years old, and she was busy cooking dinner, so she was reluctant to let me venture out. But after some persistent whining, she finally gave in.

My outdoor adventure, however, was short-lived. In just a minute outside, I caught a glimpse of a passing police car. Feeling mischievous, I stuck my tongue out at the police officer, only to see his brake lights suddenly illuminate. Fear rushed through me, and I quickly ran back indoors. To my dismay, my misbehavior earned me a sharp slap from my mother.

These were my earliest memories and marked the beginning of my life's journey in the late 1960s. My father, an Ethiopian Arab, and my Romany Gypsy mother decided to move our family to Addis Ababa, Ethiopia. Although my recollections of that time are hazy, I do remember standing in line at a school, waiting my turn in the classroom. The teacher held a wire cable in his hand and would whip any child who couldn't recite the Amharic alphabet correctly.

Fortunately, the bell rang just as it was almost my turn to face the punishment. Taking advantage of the opportunity, I swiftly escaped and raced back home. I was around seven years old, and my mother immediately withdrew me from that school upon hearing about the teacher's

actions. Instead, I had the privilege of playing and interacting with children from the Maasai tribe.

Together, we embarked on thrilling adventures, hunting and using discarded materials to create various things. We ingeniously made cups with handles using empty tomato cans, and we would sometimes go out, following the tracks of giant rock snakes in the hopes of finding one in the wild. However, our attempts were always in vain as the elusive creatures managed to elude us.

And so, these early memories shaped the foundation of my life's journey, a time when curiosity and innocence merged, leading me into a world filled with wonders and challenges that lay ahead.

As life went on, more extraordinary events unfolded. I recall a locust plague descending upon our house in a place called France Mosel tania. Millions of locusts covered everything around us, but as suddenly as they came, they dropped dead from the sky. It was an astonishing sight, and we had to use bulldozers to collect them and sell them as food in the market.

In addition to the locusts, I witnessed astonishing scenes that left me in awe and ignited my belief in magic. I saw a beggar who cut off his own tongue, and another who miraculously pushed a pole through his throat. To my amazement, both of them emerged unharmed, as if nothing had happened. It was a a testament to the inexplicable and wondrous aspects of life.

Life continued its twists and turns, and the military eventually overthrew Emperor Haile Selassie. Due to my father's connection to the palace, we had to flee Ethiopia on the very same day. Our escape led us to Egypt, where I experienced a truly magical adventure. Playing near the towering pyramids, I was mesmerized by their colossal size. It was as if I was stepping into the footprints of the gods themselves.

During our time in Egypt, which lasted about a year, suspicions arose that my father was a spy for Ethiopia, despite it being far from the truth. The mystique of Egypt and its ancient gods captivated me, influencing the book I am now writing. Within its pages, I reveal the key to unlocking and utilizing the magic that resides within each of us, regardless of our faith.

To fully comprehend the workings of magic and how to harness it, I will share my personal experiences and the lessons I have learned. As fate would have it, Hermes himself, the messenger of the gods, bestowed upon me the gift of sight and magic. With this gift, I can see things beyond the ordinary—soul mates, fairies, unicorns, and more. They are real, waiting to be seen by those who have awakened to the magic that surrounds us.

The journey you are about to embark on will

open your eyes to the true enchantment of life. It will reveal the intertwined nature of magic and reality as I narrate the unfolding story where magic played a pivotal role in real-life events. Prepare yourself to witness the wonders that have been hidden in plain sight, and allow me to be your guide in rediscovering the magic that resides within you.

Please be aware that at the time of these events, I didn't know anything about religion. My mom always told me to say it was against my beliefs when it came to religious education so I didn't have to participate. Now, looking back, I'm thankful for that. Like any religion, everyone has the right to believe what they want. We all pray to a higher power, a creator, but we may have different ideas about heaven. Still, each person's belief is valid because it's about having faith in something, not just accepting what others say. It's interesting how even religions use magic to gain power, which is kind of ironic.

I came back to the UK in the early 70s. About a year later, my parents split up, and I had to live with my dad. Unfortunately, my dad treated me badly, so I decided to run away when I was eleven. I hid in abandoned houses, and my sister secretly brought me food. I stayed hidden for about two weeks until the police found me and took me to the police station. My dad came to pick me up, but I refused to go back home. Social workers were called, and they said I couldn't stay at the police station. They offered me voluntary care, and I gladly accepted. Even though I was young, I felt mature enough to make decisions.

They sent me to a children's home called Barrow Hall, which was a big house with animals and stables. There were only a few of us, aged one to twelve, and we called the staff Uncle Robert, Auntie Mary, and so on. It was like being in one of those adventure books by Enid Blyton. Every day, I milked goats, collected duck eggs, and took care of the stables. It was amazing! I felt so free, just like when I was in Africa. There was no religion there; it was all about enjoying our freedom. But as time went on, I started missing my mom a lot. I couldn't bear being apart from her anymore, so I ran away from the children's home to find her.

Luckily, a kind lady gave me a ride while I was hitchhiking. When we reached my hometown, I saw my mom and shouted, "Stop the car, there's my mom!" I hadn't seen her for two years. At that time, it felt like a big coincidence, but now I believe it was pure magic. I had wished to see my mom, and there she was. Some might say it was just luck, but now I understand that magic played a part.

My mom took me to the gypsy site where she was living, but we realized it was risky for her to keep me there. Even though I loved being with my mom and I missed the animals at the children's home. We

decided it was best for me to go back there, and I would visit the gypsy site on weekends. It was the best of both worlds! The gypsy site was exciting. I swam in the river and dove for mussels, which my mom would pickle and sell at the pub. There were fortune-tellers and card readers, showing me glimpses of magic. I tried to use my mind to open doors and windows, but it didn't work. At that time, I didn't fully understand magic, but I was fascinated by it.

Although I didn't have religious education, I believed in Jesus. I would cross my hands over my chest, feeling sad about the terrible way he died. I had respect, sympathy, and kindness towards Jesus. Looking back, I believe Jesus and Hermes or Thoth are the same. As you read further in this book, you'll learn how Jesus or Thoth and even Lucifer use magic. I want to warn you, though, to stay away from dealing with Lucifer. He's evil. My advice is to choose Jesus, Thoth, Buddha, or Mohammed as your god, no matter what your beliefs are. Choose a loving god and use magic with kindness and care. That's what matters. You have the freedom to choose between good and evil, driven by your intentions and free will. And trust me, if you mess with demons, you'll be terrified. This book is here to guide you into a higher dimension, a place of miracles, magic, love, and kindness. It also marks the end of Satan's power.

Now let's get back to the story. But before I continue, I want to mention a little something. When I was eleven, I went to the cinema for the first time after returning from Egypt. The movie I watched was called "Jason and the Argonauts." It was an amazing epic journey that blew my mind. One moment, I was in the great pyramids, and the next, I was watching this epic film about the Greek gods. Thoth, who is Hermes in Greek mythology, was the same god. The Romans called him Mercury. So, the pyramids and "Jason and the Argonauts" were two more coincidences that I was about to embark on a magical journey. To me, it felt epic and real, even if it seems coincidental to you; hopefully, you can see and believe the same.

Life after that was pretty normal, just like any other kid. I started learning and performing magic tricks, and my friends were always impressed. But it was just for fun, and I didn't realize that real magic existed. When I was around 15, I left the children's home. My mom had to leave the caravan site and get a house so that I could come home. I stayed there for about a year and met this older girl who had a baby. I ended up leaving home again at 16 and moved in with her. Her brother didn't approve of me because he didn't want his sister dating a person of color. That's what I am: 34% Ethiopian, 1% Egyptian, 20% Scottish, 20% Romany Gypsy on the English

side, and 20% Iraqi. The rest is from Ireland and Norway, I believe. If you look at my DNA, it's another coincidence that I'm from the Levant region. At the time of writing this, everything feels coincidental. But it all ties into what happens next.

By now, I had left school, and one day while walking down the road, I saw a chopper-style 50cc motorbike in a shop window. It captivated me, and I could picture myself riding it into the sunset. So, every day, I would pass by and ask the storekeeper if I could sit on it. I loved everything about it and knew I would get it when I had enough money. I got a part-time job at a market stall and saved some money. Back in the late '70s, £400 was a lot, but I was too impatient. I ended up buying a cheaper bike. Later on, my first significant bike was a 400cc. I know you're probably wondering how this relates to magic, but bear with me; it will all make sense soon enough. I rode that bike for a while without a license and all. Then I swapped it for a 650cc chopper named "Feeling Blue." I kept it until I was about 19 years old.

During this time, I was invited to a rock party in a club with live music. I went with a group of guys who also rode bikes. We were all having a good time when one of the guys told us about his run-in with the local Hells Angels. They had left the party in a hurry, but unfortunately, my bike wouldn't start, and I was left alone. Suddenly, about ten tough-looking

Hells Angels approached me. I admit I was a bit scared. But to my surprise, they asked how I was doing and what was wrong with the bike. They helped me get it started, and it was such a relief. This encounter opened up a whole new chapter in my life because the president of the Hells Angels, who happened to be a friend of my mom through the Gypsy community, asked me if I wanted to come to a meeting and join the Hells Angels. I accepted the invitation and ultimately became a member. Once I met everyone at the meeting, and after a vote by the president, I was welcomed into the group. It was quite a feat considering it's a racially exclusive organization. Not only that, I even became an officer. I served as the treasurer and secretary. I stayed with the Hells Angels for about six years. They were a great bunch of bikers, but that's a whole different story.

After about six years, I decided to leave the Hells Angels. There was a disagreement between the president and me, and one day, I was in a pub packed with people. The president and two of his brothers were there, but they wouldn't speak to me. However, everyone else seemed fine with me, and to be honest, I wasn't too bothered by whatever issues they had. I could take care of myself. That night, I went to the restroom, unaware they had spiked my drink with twelve acid tabs. Later, I found out from the dealer that's what they had bought. I had no idea about any

of this, and this is where my life took a dramatic turn. It was the most terrifying experience I had ever endured. It was horrible, absolutely horrible. What happens next will shock you.

I left the pub, completely unaware that I had been spiked with tons of LSD. That's when I spotted a flower on the path. I bent down to pick it up, but it was like a damn hologram, so real in every way, but I couldn't grasp it. It had no form, almost like a spirit flower or something. It was bizarre, but I didn't dwell on it much. I just carried on walking home, and that's when things started to get really weird.

More and more flowers were sprouting from my feet as if some crazy magic was at play. I mean, seriously, this was real magic stuff! And it only got crazier from there. I was about halfway home when I suddenly saw King George and two other knights riding on white horses. They had these shining white hair and beards, and they were all decked out in armor. And guess what? They were the three brothers who had spiked me! I couldn't make any sense of it. I was like, "What the heck is going on? Why am I seeing this, and why can't anyone else see them?" It felt real, just as real as any other person on a horse, but I knew it couldn't be.

I rushed home to tell my girlfriend at the time about what I had just witnessed, but it was a total head-scratcher for both of us. No one knew I had been spiked, so they couldn't comprehend what I was going through. I was utterly puzzled, to say the least. But I tried my best to get on with life, or what I thought was life.

A couple of days later, it was raining, and I thought, "I wish it would stop raining and be sunny." And you won't believe what happened—the sun came out instantly, and the rain stopped! I was like, "Wait, did I just do that? How is this even possible?" So, just to test it out, I thought, "Okay, rain," and boom, it started pouring down! Then I thought, "Sunny," and just like that, the sun was back shining brightly. I couldn't wrap my head around it. I must be tripping hard or something, but it was all so real!

In my desperation to understand what was going on, I decided to see if these events were coincidental. So, I thought of a robin, and right away, one landed at my feet. I was convinced this was some divine sign, like a god or something was trying to tell me something religious. I felt this urge to speak to someone about it, to find some answers. So I headed to the church that had a statue of Jesus on the cross, the one where I used to pray with my arms crossed.

I knocked on the door, and the vicar answered, chewing on a damn chicken leg! I tried my best to explain what I was experiencing, thinking it might have some biblical meaning. Maybe I was the second coming or something wild like that! But all he said was,

go see a doctor." I mean, seriously, why was he turning me away like that? I was just looking for some help, for some understanding!

Churches were meant to provide guidance, especially in times of confusion about religion and acts of god, so I was hugely disappointed and speechless. Straight away, this priest turned into a sinister character who seemed to want to steal my soul. Feeling uneasy, I left the church immediately. He reminded me a bit of the Mormon guy in Poltergeist, which was creepy. However, I was still tripping on acid at that time, and the hallucinations were becoming more intense.

Feeling troubled by what I was experiencing, I decided to go to a Baptist church and share my thoughts with the priest. I believed I might be the second coming or something extraordinary due to the unnatural things I was witnessing. I was still unsure about what was happening, but my mind remained clear. The priest asked me if I had any proof, and the only thing that came to mind was a verse from the Bible warning about the second coming being like a thief in the night. However, he countered by mentioning the warning about false prophets, which made me quiet down.

Feeling anxious about being misunderstood or seen as a bad person or a Satan worshiper, I asked the priest to baptize me in the name of the Father, the Son, and the Holy Ghost, as I believed that's what I was meant to be. He cautioned me that this request was blasphemous and that I should leave. Feeling upset and worried, my once beautiful trip with flowers, birds, and sunshine started turning into a nightmarish experience. Despite the challenges, I was determined to find answers and headed to a third church. The priest there wasn't very knowledgeable about my experiences and suggested I talk to four Franciscan monks who lived in the house I used to play in as a child.

Before visiting the monks, I decided to prepare myself, still under the influence of acid. I thought about having the sun come out, and to my amazement, it appeared again. As I knocked on the monks' door, a monk greeted me and mentioned he could see that I brought autumn with me, confirming that he perceived the same magical things I did. Inside, he asked me peculiar questions about my family, making me uncomfortable and uneasy.

During our conversation, the monk pointed to a cluster of seven eggcups and asked if I knew what they represented. My mind went to the mother goose and the golden egg, and he confirmed it was somewhat related. I was asked to stay in touch, and after a few days, a realization struck me, and I phoned the monk again. He clarified that one of the eggs represented gloom, and the church would agree with that

interpretation. His name was Brother Anselm.

Upon hearing this, the pieces fell into place, and the egg cups' message became clear. The name "Salem" formed in my mind as a warning. I panicked, realizing that I was being associated with witchcraft and witch hunters, which could put my life in danger. I rushed back home, but on my way I heard haunting drum sounds, which made me curious. I found the witch hunter general and his men waiting for me, with my family and friends tied to stakes on bonfires, as if they were about to be executed. They saw us as magic people who needed to be suppressed and eliminated to secure the church's power.

To escape this terrifying illusion, I had to convince myself it wasn't real. I focused on happy thoughts, making the vision fade away.

I noticed that if I got scared about something, my fear would bring it to life. However, if I told myself it was not real and thought of something else, it went away. So, I was starting to gain some control over what was happening. But it was at this point that I started to get really scared. I now had the witch hunter on my case, and I began to realize that these church guys might be involved in something sinister. My terror only made the hallucinations more powerful.

One day, about six months later, a friend noticed my condition and took me to the hospital. I was delirious by then and had lost all touch with reality. They admitted me to a psychiatric ward, where I was given a large dose of Liegactill, commonly called liquid Cosh, to calm me down. In that state, I sat in the nut house staring at a telephone, trying to move it with my mind because I couldn't control my arms. I desperately wanted to call my mom. I remained in this state for about a week until the hallucinations began to subside, or at least, I thought they were stopping.

Feeling relieved and thinking things were back to normal, I mustered the courage to go to the dining hall for something to eat. But as I started eating a strange thought popped into my head – the food tasted weird, and the carrots looked like fingers. And just as I had that thought, they transformed into chopped-off fingers, like a scene from a horror movie. I turned around, and to my horror, all the patients in the dining hall turned into ghastly flesh-eating creatures. The sight was terrifying, and I ended up throwing up. From then on, I refused to eat, fearing more disturbing visions.

One day, an orderly male nurse came up behind me, put my arm up my back, and forced me into the dining room, insisting that I eat. It was a humiliating experience, but there was no way I could eat anything with the hallucinations still tormenting me. The medication was starting to suppress the fear, though, and after about a month, I began to feel more stable and back in touch with reality, or at least as close as I could get.

As I left the hospital, calm and composed, I asked myself, "What the heck was all that?" The acid no longer seemed to have an effect on me, and things seemed normal. I was diagnosed with schizophrenia and treated accordingly with daily injections, but it seemed to be working. The hallucinations stopped, and I felt immense relief. Strangely, I still heard voices, but the doctors kept giving me injections until the voices eventually stopped. It was a bizarre experience to go through. Schools and religion teach you to reach out to Jesus, that He will come to you. But the doctors told me not to hear those voices, and they kept giving me injections until they stopped.

I settled back home, but as I sat down, I couldn't shake the disturbing thoughts from the priest's warnings about the false prophet and the actions of the witch-hunter general. I started to contemplate what if I was the devil because I believed in magic. However, I reassured myself that I wasn't satanic; I was kind and humble, as anyone who knew me would say. Nevertheless, the thoughts persisted, and soon, visions of vampires and werewolves flooded my mind. Astonishingly, as soon as I thought, "Shit, I'm a werewolf," my body went into spasms as if I was transforming into one. It scared me even more, and my girlfriend called the doctors, who rushed in and gave me another jab. The spasms ceased, and my body returned to normal. The doctors explained it as a side effect of the medication, but deep down, I felt that it was more than that.

You're probably wondering what schizophrenia has to do with magic. Schizophrenia is a term used to describe the following:

- Hallucinations are seeing or hearing things that do not exist outside of the mind.
- Delusions-unusual beliefs that are not based on reality.
- People with schizophrenia do not have a split personality.
- Schizophrenia does not usually cause someone to be violent.

So, in retrospect, the effects of LSD and schizophrenia seemed similar. It was at this point that I realized I had been spiked with something. Others who knew me confirmed it. I wondered about the quantity and the person responsible. While a bit upset, I felt relieved to understand that it was all due to acid hallucinations. I told the doctor about my acid use during my next visit, but they dismissed it, claiming it wouldn't stay in my system for long. However, I knew otherwise, as it has been 40 years, and I still experience hallucinations to this day.

This all started at the beginning of the first year, and the visions persisted. It's like a magic ability, allowing me to see anything I desire and materialize things in both the spirit world and the 3D world. I believe this power resides within all of us. And it's not all frightening, so I urge you to continue reading as it gets truly magical. After finishing this book, you'll be amazed by what you can see too.

I gradually understood it was all hallucinations, but some aspects remained puzzling. For instance, why did I see the three brothers as King George and the witch hunter, who turned out to be the hospital doctors? It was incredibly bizarre. I began to contemplate the existence of other states of reality. For instance, I encountered a woman who claimed to be my mother and asked me to take my pills. However, she looked nothing like my real mom and seemed like a completely different person. I suspected she intended to harm me and stopped taking the medication based on this belief.

About a year later, I moved to a big city with a cathedral. This frightened me because I still believed that churches were trying to eradicate our magic and were out to catch me. Despite that, I learned to tune them out when they got too close. I now recognize this as a gift and must tread carefully.

One day, while about to take a bath, I heard a voice that I could only describe as a god. It told me not to move, as the fate of mankind depended on it. I was at a critical point of no return, with one foot in the bath and the other on the floor. If I stepped into the bath, it would lead to the undoing of creation, as both poles, negative and positive, would be in the same place. Similarly, if I stepped out, it would have dire consequences. I stood there frozen for about six hours until the thought dissipated, and I was able to laugh at myself and step out of the bath.

Next, I heard another voice that I believed was god's, stating that the world was going to end as part of a rebirth and awakening. I had a massive vision of a zombie holocaust that terrified me. It seemed so real that I panicked and thought it was truly awful. Walking up the street one day, I thought I saw one of them, and by the time I reached the top of the street, everyone had turned into zombies, and I was the only survivor. This was no longer just in my head; it became my reality, and I've experienced this vision numerous times. I realized that if I feared them, they would become real, but by remaining calm, they would pass by me. Unfortunately, I doubted myself, made eye contact with one, and they chased after me. I managed to escape, running up to a sloping wall with zombies in pursuit. There was a hatch leading to an attic in the building adjoining the wall. As the zombies closed in, I realized I was hallucinating again; this wasn't real. I was halfway through the

hatch, trying to escape, when one grabbed my leg, and I shouted to wake myself up. I knew I was in another realm of reality, and through that hatch, I could escape into another world. I continued shouting until my partner woke me up, and I found myself back in bed, away from the zombie-filled arena.

I asked her why it took her so long to wake me up, and she told me it was the strangest thing she had ever witnessed. Apparently, I had been shouting in my sleep, begging to be awakened, and yet, I had left home that day and encountered the zombies. But miraculously, I had woken up in bed, escaping from them. It was an unexplainable phenomenon, and I couldn't comprehend how I was capable of such a thing.

I had a realization that the churches were conjuring demonic imagery to instill deep fear within me so that I would surrender to them. But I wasn't one to be defeated, especially when the fate of mankind was at stake. I had to act quickly, as I firmly believed that the end of the world would manifest as a zombie holocaust due to the power of fear and the ability to materialize it into reality. The magic was unbelievably potent.

For about five years, I continued to have premonitions of zombies every night. I also had visions of a great flood, where I could see myself helping people onto a boat. Both the zombies and the flooding disturbed me greatly, but the medication kept them from becoming my reality. I began to grasp how things worked and how I could transition in and out of different realms of reality at will. There were numerous dimensions to explore.

Driven by dissatisfaction with the doctors' explanations, I delved into researching the workings of the mind. I studied hypnosis and psychology, and during my studies and while on medication, I found that they helped keep most of my visions and premonitions at bay. Keeping my mind focused on my studies proved to be beneficial.

It was during this period that I discovered the pineal gland, also known as the third eye, and its role in vision. I learned that the Egyptians were aware of this and referred to it as the Eye of Horus. The shape of the pineal gland resembled the drawings in the pyramids. The Egyptians utilized it to see other dimensions, similar to my experiences. This led me to contemplate Hermes or Thoth, who suddenly came to mind. I sensed that the voices in my head were from Hermes, but I needed confirmation.

Strangely enough, on the same day, a friend visited me and recommended a book called "Hermetica," written by Hermes 2000 years ago. I devoured the entire book in a single day, astonished by the coincidental timing of my friend's suggestion. The book opened up a whole new realm of understanding

for me. I went on to read the Emerald Tablets, which were pure magic. As I delved deeper, my visions took on a new significance, and fear began to dissipate. The mysteries were gradually unraveling before me.

With newfound courage, I decided to stop running from the darkness and actively seek out Hermes. Everything I thought of seemed to manifest in real life, so I sat quietly in a chair, closed my eyes, and embarked on a quest to find Hermes. I astral traveled to what could only be described as the outer limits of our imagination, even traversing through an infinite black void. I repeated this practice daily for months until, one day, as if by magic, I encountered him. He was sitting in the same position as the thinking man statue, sobbing. I asked if he was Hermes, and he confirmed it. Curious about his distress, I inquired why he was crying. He replied, "Nobody believes in magic anymore, so everything is fading into nothing." That's when I assured him, "I believe in you. That's how I found you."

Hermes sat there, looking at me, and explained that all it took to restore the magic was to believe in its reality. Given the life I had experienced, how could I not believe in its existence? I was aware that I was hallucinating, so I thought if I can hallucinate zombies, then I can hallucinate Hermes. The excitement of this magical revelation surged through me.

In an instant, Hermes illuminated and flew away,

urging me to follow him. He guided me out of the bewildering maze of altered realities known as the abyss or the matrix. We stood together on the edge of the abyss, with Hermes perched on a rock beside me. He instructed me to sit and wait. As a thick fog passed by, dissipating into the air, a colossal fortress wall emerged. It was immense, impenetrable—neither scalable nor circumventable. In the centre stood the entrance, guarded by the colossal figure of Anubis. He did not move or speak audibly; instead, our communication occurred through telepathy.

Anubis weighed my heart and mind, evaluating my essence. If I passed this test, I would be allowed to venture beyond him. I expressed my desire to explore what lay beyond the entrance, but Anubis explained that I couldn't pass for two reasons: first, I was still alive, and second, I belonged to a mixed race. However, he reassured me, stating that I would reside in the realms of Hermes, both in the upper world and the lower world. Similar to Hermes, I would have the ability to traverse different realms at will. I was filled with excitement and gratitude, as this prospect was far better than facing a dreadful death. After spending some time there, feeling content with Anubis's words, I returned back to my physical body.

Eager to deepen my understanding of these gods, I embarked on the study of hieroglyphics. I achieved distinction in reading and writing them. Although I

haven't read any hieroglyphic texts yet, I plan to do so on my next visit to Egypt. I am curious to read them directly from the pyramids. This study has granted me a profound comprehension of how Hermes communicates and imparts his magic and wisdom. It's important to note that religions often employ hermetic teachings and magic, yet they withhold the knowledge of how it truly works.

Now that I had found a companion in Hermes (or Jesus, for the sake of this discussion), I started to feel calmer and focused on positive thoughts. It took a few months to recover from my past ordeals, but I eventually delved back into my mind through self-hypnosis, seeking to connect with Hermes once again. And there he was, appearing before me. I expressed my concerns, stating that I was just one man, and the churches possessed all the magical artifacts, including the emerald tablets, which they were using for nefarious purposes against humanity. How could I, a mere mortal, do anything against such odds?

Hermes assured me not to fear, acknowledging the truth of the situation. However, he advised that I needn't worry about the physical possession of the emerald tablets, as they were present within each of us. All we had to do was believe in their reality, and the magic would activate automatically. I had always sensed that we possessed an internal book of magic, but I hadn't fully understood its nature. Nevertheless,

I had uncovered much of its essence: an internal bible, a divine gift bestowed upon all of us, regardless of our faith. It resided within our DNA. Religion had kept us from realizing our own inherent magic, perpetuating false beliefs. We needed to embrace and believe in our own magic, which exists within each and every one of us.

A few years passed, and I found myself living a somewhat normal life. Everything was starting to make sense. What I had once perceived as hallucinations and schizophrenia turned out to be pure magic, the finest alchemy. Imagine being able to interact with gods, traverse dimensions, and witness things that others couldn't comprehend. Surely, that was the essence of magic. But let me tell you, there was even more to it.

During the COVID-19 pandemic, the Lion's Gate alignment occurred in the constellations. This celestial gate was governed by Anubis and Sirius. Determined not to be confined to my flat during the lockdown, I purchased a cheap boat and headed to Scotland. I spent eight months there, enduring harsh winter conditions and 70-mile gales—quite the ordeal. I remember one stormy day when my brother and partner arrived. As my brother slipped on the pontoon, I rushed to help him up. At that moment, the sky flashed yellow, and the sun radiated an extraordinary brilliance. It was a stormy day, yet

right before my eyes, the vision of flooding that I had seen previously unfolded. I couldn't comprehend what was happening. We walked up the pontoon together, but as I reached the pontoon gate, I felt myself return to my physical body. The gates to other dimensions closed within my mind. Anubis and Hermes had guided me out of the abyss and back to reality. From that moment on, fear ceased to exist within me.

Once again, I sought out Hermes and questioned him about the visions of zombies I had experienced. He explained that in order for mankind to awaken to the fifth dimension, there had to be an ending—an end to the cycle of war and pestilence. The COVID-19 pandemic, as it turned out, was the most humane way to bring about this transformation. It was a realization that validated my years of seeing visions of zombies, which now manifested as a COVID holocaust. However, in this case, the "zombies" were not physical biters but rather individuals who unknowingly transmitted the virus through sneezing and close contact. The lockdown and containment measures aligned with what I had envisioned. Now, everything was starting to make sense.

We are now entering the Age of Aquarius, the golden age, and transitioning into the fifth dimension. In this realm, we can imagine and experience anything we desire, encountering magical places and phenomena. I have already awakened to fifth-dimension. In this realm, we can imagine and experience anything we desire, encountering magical places and phenomena. I have already awakened to fifth-dimensional thinking, propelled by the effects of acid, although the process would have been less daunting and frightening if it had occurred naturally. But fear not, my friends, for you need not endure the same journey I did. You have the opportunity to evolve naturally and embrace the real magic that awaits in the fifth dimension.

Before I continue the rest of the story, there's a little more to share. Despite having better thoughts, I still lived in fear of the churches and the demonic entities I saw. I felt compelled to confront Lucifer, which was scary, but I knew I had to do it. I focused my mind, and once again, I journeyed out of my body through time and space, determined to see Lucifer face-to-face.

As I approached him, I encountered horrifying images of demonic, vampire-like figures, but I pushed past them, refusing to be scared. I even smelled death and rotting corpses, but I pressed on. Soon, I faced three ugly witches with no eyes, only eyes in their hands. They screamed at me, warning me that no mortal had ever reached this place and urged me to turn back or be doomed. Undeterred, I told them to get lost and continued forward.

The fog appeared again, but this time, Anubis

wasn't there to greet me. It was Lucifer himself, just as I had seen in movies—ugly with horns and red skin. I told him he didn't scare me and that his reign was over. I refused to follow him and suggested he should hand his powers over to Hermes. He tried to deceive me, claiming he was a product of our imagination, shaped by how the world perceived him. He stated that he never asked to be born this way, and if we desired, we could paint him a new face in our imagination.

I pondered his words, but in the end, I stood by my original thought that good is good, and evil is evil—no trickery involved. As I knew that most churches were Luciferian, I decided to stick with Hermes and leave Lucifer be, recognizing that his power was diminishing as more people woke up and rejected evil.

After Hermes returned me to my body and my third eye closed, I witnessed the sky lighting up again. It was a breathtaking sight while I was sitting in a restaurant. Everyone there was taking photos of the unusual storm with intense lightning. To me, it represented the epic battle between Hermes and Lucifer, with Hermes preventing Lucifer from entering our 3D world.

Overwhelmed, I hurried to the hospital and got more medication, not wanting to experience any more frightening visions. I spent about two weeks in the hospital, where astonishing events began to unfold. Suddenly, the hospital transformed into a spaceship—it was Hermes' spaceship. The nurses turned into the ship's crew, and I realized that I was the captain of this space vessel. I felt like I was truly in outer space, understanding that Earth itself was like a spaceship in the vast cosmos. I didn't need a spacesuit to venture outside, as my mind was wide open to these grand possibilities.

While sitting in this spaceship, I marveled at the incredible experience. Eventually, a door opened, and I walked into what was known as the Halls of Amente, located in the 6th dimension. It was a place where I could rest and feel safe. Remarkably, the hospital was named Safe Haven, which seemed fitting. I spent a few hours in this magical place before encountering a girl with fangs and pointed ears. She sang the most beautiful songs and introduced me to a younger guy who immediately said, "Hi, I'm Poseidon." Our connection was instant as we discovered we had much in common.

The next day, I had a conversation with a priest about St. Columba. I asked if he was the man who had a crystal book inside him and was made a saint. The priest confirmed this, and I confronted him about St. Columba's violent past of rape, plunder, and killing of women and children. The priest's response was that things were different back in those days. I

I challenged him, saying that the only difference was that my book, the emerald green one, didn't condone such violence.

Just then, the girl with fangs and pointed ears rushed in, distressed about what she called the rapture happening outside. I immediately knew what she meant and told her not to fear Lucifer, as that's what he wanted. I reassured her that surrendering was what he desired. The priest seemed unsure about how to react to the situation.

I was discharged from the hospital on the day of the COP26 rally in Glasgow. I went there with a billboard around my neck, warning that the end was nigh, but surprisingly, no one paid attention. I returned home, relieved to be out of the hospital, leaving Hermes to battle it out with Lucifer, unsure of the outcome.

The real magic I experienced goes beyond tricks—it involves true sorcery, witchcraft, and alchemy, with the power to materialize anything you can imagine. I explained everything that happened to show how I found the lost wisdom of the gods.

Now, if you want to know how to use this magic for good, you don't need to go through what I experienced. You can access it more naturally and safely. Allow me to introduce you to the Magic Book of Cadabra - my personal magic book, my magic heaven. "Abracadabra" and "So mote it be" are powerful magical phrases that mean "as it is written, so it shall be." The name Cadabra felt fitting for this book. It contains the wisdom and magic that lies within us all, our internal magic book, Bible, or Quran. We don't need to read someone else's vision of divinity—God is inside each one of us.

When you truly believe, you can speak to god, regardless of your faith. But the key is genuine belief in the reality of the divine presence within you.

The magic happens like this: have you ever thought about someone and they suddenly called you? And when you mentioned that you were just thinking of them, they confirmed it wasn't a coincidence? Well, it's not merely chance. Your magic book influenced them to reach out to you. The same goes for walking down the street and thinking of someone, only to have them approach you. It's not another coincidence—it's more magic.

These examples can go on and on. Many people talk about manifestation and raising vibrations, but it doesn't work like that. You must believe with absolute conviction as if there's no tomorrow. I've given you two examples of how magic can materialize a phone call and bring a person into your presence. You can apply this to anything. For instance, I was feeling a bit down when entering a swimming centre, and I casually said, "Wish I had a wand to make it all stop." I didn't think much of it. But on my way out,

I noticed a stick on the floor, about 30 inches long, with the bark removed and a little bend at the end for holding. It looked like a wand to me. So, thank you, Lord Thoth.

When you truly believe in the reality of your your inner magic, it comes to life. Religions have conditioned us to suppress it, but it's your personal Bible—it's within you. There's no need to be afraid; it's an integral part of who you are.

Here are some more examples: Have you ever wished to see a robin while looking around your garden, and suddenly one appears? Most would consider it a mere coincidence, but you're mistaken. All you need to do is imagine a robin in your internal magic book and say, "Abracadabra, please send me a robin." Within half an hour, one will come right up to you. There's no limit to your creative imagination. You can ask for anything. Here's another example: say "Abracadabra, please send me my soul mate," and vividly imagine them on a page in your internal magic book. Be as detailed as you want. Then, go for a walk into town, and I guarantee you will encounter your soul mate, just like when you unexpectedly meet a friend. It's no longer coincidental—it's magic on demand.

So, get creative with your mind and conjure up as much goodness as you can. There's no limit. I've noticed that the book of magic works in mysterious ways, just like the divine. Let's say you want a new car, and you make a wish to your magic book for money to buy it. On the same day, you might see an advertisement on TV, on your phone, or even in the street, offering a new car with no interest, deposit, or low payments. It will happen on the same day you ask for it. Or, if you want money for fishing tackle to go fishing, you might come across an advertisement saying, "Make money from home fishing." It may seem strange, but that's how it works.

Have you ever thought that it's as if the computer can read your mind? Whenever you think of something, it pops up on your computer. Well, again, it's not a coincidence. Your magic book is constantly reading your mind and heart, 24/7. But you didn't know that you were manifesting everything by magic. Now is your chance to consciously ask and take note of how many coincidences you experience in just one day. Once you reach the point of realizing that these can't be mere coincidences, you're on the right path to believing in your magic.

I'll share with you a couple of examples where real miracles happened. I met a new partner, and 8 weeks into the relationship, we received devastating news after she had an X-ray. She was diagnosed with terminal cancer, and given about 5 weeks to live. She had stage 4 cancer with a massive tumor in her chest, measuring 13 by 11 by 8 inches. As the weeks passed, her condition deteriorated to the point where

she needed assistance to move in and out of bed. It seemed like she was sadly reaching the end of her life.

Feeling desperate, I went outside and sat on a bench, reaching out to Hermes once again, seeking his magical help. In tears, I suddenly witnessed about 300 crows flying around the sky and landing in the tree next to me. I knew this was a sign; crows symbolize medicine and magic. Although I feared she might pass away that day, the telephone rang, and the hospital asked us to come in. To our astonishment, the consultant apologized, stating they had misdiagnosed my partner. Instead of terminal cancer, she had non-Hodgkin's lymphoma cancer, which was treatable. The odds of such a misdiagnosis turning into a treatable condition were miraculous indeed.

She immediately started chemo and radiotherapy, but further complications arose, including pneumonia, leading to three instances in intensive care with life support. On the third occasion, her one good lung filled with fluid, and she decided not to be resuscitated if she fell into a coma. Tragically, she did fall into a coma, and I felt it was the end of the road.

Seeking solace, I went to a spiritual house that had once been Emperor Haile Selassie's spiritual home during his exile in Britain. There, I met a Rasta priest and shared my ordeal. He confidently assured me that she would be okay. Filled with the belief in magic, I rushed back to the hospital. Her doctor was waiting in the corridor, uncertain about what to do as she had requested not to be resuscitated. Despite this, he acknowledged that she had a fighting chance. I passionately pleaded with him to resuscitate her, and he agreed. Miraculously, she was brought back from the coma.

Today, I'm pleased to say she is completely cancer-free, having been in remission for over 10 years. Her chances are now the same as anyone else's, and she enjoys activities like swimming in the sea with dolphins. These are not mere coincidences but the result of miracles and magic. For those who may still be skeptical, don't worry; it's a part of your awakening process. As you notice these occurrences in your life, you are getting closer to embracing the magic within. I'll teach you the best way to communicate with those who have passed over, such as your grandparents.

If you want to see and communicate with someone who has passed away, it's quite simple. Just sit down, close your eyes, take three deep breaths, and exhale slowly. Then, ask your magic book to reveal your secret magic garden to you. In your imagination, visualize a beautiful, magical garden filled with vibrant flowers, buzzing insects, and an ornate bench. Feel the warmth of the sun on your skin as you notice an ornate gate at the end of the

garden. You can hear joyful laughter coming from behind the gate, but you are not permitted to go there as it's not yet your time. However, the good news is that your departed loved ones can come to you. Reach out to the person you wish to connect with, ask them to come, and they will indeed appear. You can sit together, have a conversation, say your goodbyes, and stay for as long as you wish. Believe in the reality of this magic, for when you dismiss it, you dismiss your connection with your ancestors.

Now, let me show you how to keep demons out of your mind, as they are also real. Follow the same steps as before: close your eyes, take three deep breaths, and exhale slowly. Turn to your inner Bible and request it to show you your alchemy library, remembering to say "Abracadabra" before making any wishes or requests. Imagine yourself standing in front of a door with a table beside it. Visualize a magic key appearing on the table. This key is unique to you, and only you can decide who enters with you. Use the key to unlock the door and enter your alchemy library.

In the library, you'll find books on the left representing the negative aspects of your life and on the right, the positive ones. Locate the book titled "Demons and Excuses" on the left side and take it off the shelf. Open the book and see all your demons listed within its pages. Then, walk to the basement of the library, where you'll find a fire furnace. Toss the book into the furnace and watch it burn to ashes, feeling a sense of relief as you let go of your demons. Return to the main library area and find another table. Imagine a new book appearing on the table. as if by magic. This book is called "My Health and Happiness." Place this book on the shelf where the demon book was. Repeat this process with all the negative books, replacing them with new magical and inspirational ones. Keep doing this until your entire library is filled with books of magic, dreams, and wishes. You'll find great joy in this place once you get the hang of it, just like with the magical garden.

These are genuine, real magic places that you can experience today. I hope this book has opened your eyes to the reality of magic and inspired you to revive your imaginary friends. Remember, the world is infinite, and all that I've shared is just a tiny grain of sand in the vast ocean of possibilities. Embrace the magic within you and explore the wonders it can bring to your life.

MAGIC
MAGIC BOK

A note from the author

I deliberately saved this part for the end because the person I want to give more recognition to is my mother. As you may recall, I've pledged allegiance to Hermes, but my mother's role in my life is equally heroic and essential. Back when we lived in Ethiopia, my mother, a Romany gipsy lady, used to write stories for us to read.

While Hermes has been the inspiration behind this book, my mother holds a special place in my heart because when I found myself struggling with the demons, I reached out to her, even though she had sadly passed away. Despite her physical absence, she would appear to me in visions, guiding and supporting me, much like a magic typewriter typing me out of difficult situations. It truly felt like a collaborative effort, involving me, my mother, and Hermes.

Now, do you grasp the reality of magic? Regardless of whether you refer to it as Jesus and your book as the Bible, or follow the Quran, it's all the same magic. The core principles are universal, and it's about connecting with the genuine version inside you, your personal holy book. No matter your faith, the magic resides within.

This is your life, and it's your magic; embrace it, let it shine, and illuminate your path. The light of your magic is arriving, guiding you towards enlightenment and growth.

Let's explore the difference between religion and magic: magic draws its divine inspiration from our internal holy book of magic. It's a personal, intrinsic connection to the divine. Religion, on the other hand, gets its divine inspiration from a priest or religious authorities who write down and often alter teachings to suit their needs. In some cases, it may lead to a dogmatic approach that bombards the mind rather than fostering a genuine spiritual connection.

Remember, magic is authentic, innate, and a beautiful aspect of life, while religion, when misused, can lose its true essence and spiritual depth. Embrace the magic within you and let it guide you to a profound understanding of the world around you.

I Now Know Who I am; I am magic.

Everything in life is an optical illusion. Did the tree fall, or did we imagine? It fell like perception is essential to magic being real, So I won't be returning to religion. I am staying with the people experiencing poverty. Wouldn't it be good if everybody believed me when I said magic is real?

A famous quote by Bob Marley

Emancipate yourself from mental slavery
None but ourselves can free our mind

This is the first book of a trilogy.
Book two: "The Battle of Cadabra"
Book three: "The Cadabra"

www.ingramcontent.com/pod-product-compliance
Lightning Source LLC
LaVergne TN
LVHW041202080426
835511LV00006B/707
9781739512231